Eph. 6:10-12
Isah. 43:1—:

EFFECTIVE PRAYER STRATEGIES

If we Beleve The word of God our Body will
Stay Healed.
We are not belleving what The word Say

EFFECTIVE PRAYER STRATEGIES

8 Principles for A Powerful Prayer Life

FELECIA CARTER WADE

Effective Prayer Strategies, 8 Principles for a Powerful Prayer Life
Copyright © 2021 by Felecia Carter Wade
First Edition: November 2021

Chief Editor: Deborah G. Hunter
Book cover design: BLLP Firm, bllpfirm.com, email: contact@bllpfirm.com

ISBN: 979-8-9850586-0-4
Printed in the United States of America.

Dedication

This book is dedicated to…
Everyone who has ever prayed for me!

"The effectual fervent prayers of a righteous man availeth much."

— James 5:16, KJV

Acknowledgements

I would not be doing what I'm called to do successfully without the help of intercessors. To the prophetic intercessors at my home church, *Divine Life Church* in Memphis, thank you for your commitment to pray for me, call on me, push me, and pull from me. You are a huge reason why I felt compelled to write this book. I needed to put in writing the revelations from your many questions, experiences, and zealous intuitions. I'm forever grateful for all of you. Stay on the wall!

To my amazing husband, Apostle Tony Wade, you are my general, my example, my everything. I can't even begin to explain how your force in the Spirit has pulled me up, grew me up, and sped me up. You are a great stretcher. Just when I thought I couldn't possibly be stretched any thinner, you give me another pull. I'm so grateful for you. God has used you to sharpen me in so many ways. I love you dearly.

To my two daughters, Tonecia and Soteria, you are a huge part of my inspiration to succeed at everything the Lord assigns me to do. I know you're watching me near and from afar, and I want you to see that all things are possible to those who believe. You can attain anything the Lord calls you to, and I decree that you WILL attain everything assigned to your life. I'm so Godly proud of you both. I love you dearly.

To my Lord and Savior Jesus Christ, I honor You for all You have done through my little life. I am honored that You would choose me to carry Your secrets, trust me to process them in prayer, and use me to stand in the gap for nations.

For more information on other books and products, go to www.feleciawade.com and sign up to become a VIP Warrior. Follow me on all of my social media platforms @feleciacarterwade for group studies, teachings, and live prayer.

Table of Contents

INTRODUCTION

The moment I received the baptism of the Holy Spirit, I became intrigued by the things of the Spirit. The presence of God, angels, supernatural experiences, etc. all created an unexplainable hunger within me. I didn't grow up going to church and I wasn't introduced to the supernatural power of God until I got born again in my early 20's. I do, however, remember one particular event that I was exposed to that piqued my interest and brought an element of curiosity about God. When I was a little girl, I heard my grandmother upstairs shouting, crying, and speaking in this language that scared the living daylights out of me. I asked my aunt what was wrong with my grandma, and she simply brushed it off as if it was nothing.

Once I became a believer and learned of the many ways to pray, I understood that my grandmother was upstairs praying for her seed in her heavenly language. That was pretty much the gist of my experience of the supernatural as a child. I do believe that this book and the fact that I have a heart for prayer, is because of the prayers of my Spirit-filled grandmother. Early in my salvation, the Lord started nudging me in the middle of the night to get up and pray. I didn't understand what He was preparing me for then and I most certainly didn't like losing sleep knowing I had two busy children to attend to. Holy Father was preparing me to become the intercessor I am today. I want to say to those who feel as if they don't have time to pray, the Lord already knows what's on your plate when He calls you to do things that are uncomfortable for you. He knows what's ahead of you and the amazing impact He wants from your life. It's your responsibility to yield and give Him your *yes*. I can say, now that my girls are all grown and I have a pretty flexible but still busy schedule, I look forward to the nudges from Holy Spirit. Be encouraged and know that He is looking for someone who will make a spiritual sacrifice in order to get Heaven's will done on the Earth. Prayer and obedience will move the Kingdom. More importantly, effective prayer and obedience will advance the Kingdom. My prayer is that this book will inspire you, encourage you, and push you into another dimension of prayer.

CHAPTER 1
TABERNACLE PRAYER

I t is very important to understand how to approach God in prayer. We serve a holy God. He is a righteous King. He is deserving of honor, glory, and praise every single moment of the day. So much so that there are angels surrounding His throne exclaiming, "Holy, holy, holy," exalting His reverential essence.

> *"And the four living creatures, each of them with six wings, are full of eyes all around and within, and day and night they never cease to say, "Holy, Holy, Holy, is the Lord God Almighty, who was and is and is to come!" Revelation 4:8*

In Exodus 25, God instructed Moses to construct a place where He could dwell among the Israelites. This place was called the *Tabernacle*. The Israelites could go and worship there; however, there were many important components to the tabernacle. It consisted of three main areas, the Outer Court, the Holy Place, and the Holy of Holies. This place is where the priest would go before God to get another year of mercy for the sins of the people of Israel. You may ask, what does this have to do with my prayer life today? Or you may be thinking, how does this relate to me because that was an old covenant practice and I'm under the new covenant. I can understand that train of thought because I thought the same way for many years. When I received revelation of the many important principles of prayer including this principle of tabernacle praying, I became more confident and effective in my prayers. When we understand all of the details of the tabernacle, the purpose of each court, and the reason for each piece of furniture, we will see the significance of the priestly process. Understanding the significance of the tabernacle back then is an important key to understand how we, as born-again believers, should approach a holy God and pray effectively. One of the reasons why the tabernacle principle is still relevant to us today is because we, as born-again believers, are now the temple, the sanctuary, and tabernacle of the Holy Spirit.

> *"What? know ye not that your body is the temple of the Holy Ghost which is in you, which ye have of God, and ye are not your own?"* 1 *Corinthians 6:19*

The Holy Spirit of God lives inside of us.

> *"The Spirit of God, who raised Jesus from the dead, lives in you. And just as God raised Christ Jesus from the dead, he will give life to your mortal bodies by this same Spirit living within you."* Romans 8:11

Our new regenerated spirit causes us to be one with the Holy One. Our souls (mind, will, emotions) represent the Holy Place and our bodies represent the Outer Court of the Tabernacle.

To be effective in prayer, we must go beyond our physical feelings (outer courts) as well as our own intellect (The Holy Place), but we must pray from the Spirit-realm (Holy of Holies). I call this Spirit-led prayer.

Just as the priest would enter the tabernacle into the outer court, then the brazen altar and lastly go behind the veil, our prayers should resemble this process. Ordinarily, my initial time in prayer resembles the priestly process in that I always enter God's presence with praise and thanksgiving.

"Enter into His gates with thanksgiving, and into his courts with praise: be thankful unto him, and bless his name." Psalm 100:4

I start my prayer time by thanking God for who He is and for all He has done. I begin to extol Him by telling Him of His amazing greatness. Here is an example of how I start in the outer courts of prayer: "Father, how excellent is Your name. You are Almighty and I honor You. You are the one true God and besides You, there is no other. You are the self-existing one. The one who holds time in His hand. Thank You for being faithful. Thank You for Your unconditional love. You love me with an unfailing love. Your very essence is love and You will never fail me. Mighty are You Lord. You are holy and worthy of my praises forever more. Thank You for Your Son Jesus and all that He did for me on the Cross. Jesus, You are the mighty King of kings and Lord of lords. You are the alpha and the omega. You are the beginning and the end. You are the author and finisher of my faith. You are the Creator of all things and without You, nothing would exist. You are the Lamb of God, the risen King, and the one who is to come with victory in Your hand. Forever are You worthy to be praised and I will praise Your name forever. You are my Lord and Savior and I worship You."

I can remember a time when I needed worship music every time I would enter into prayer to help me focus on God. As I began to mature in my personal prayer time, I gave the Holy Father the fruit of my own lips that flowed from my heart, rather than a songwriter's heart. Don't get me wrong, there is absolutely nothing wrong with worship music in your personal prayer time; however, I believe it's really important to allow yourself to go to a place in the Spirit where you hear your own heart's cry for the one you love and worship. Weaning yourself off of having to need worship music will be a bit uncomfortable initially, but push past the laziness of your flesh that came from always allowing the music to do the work for you. You will then begin to find yourself singing a new song to the Lord from sweet melodies flowing from your own heart.

After I finish with my time of praise and worship, I turn my focus on the blood of Jesus. Jesus' blood is what gives us access to come before the presence of a Holy God. I begin to repent of any sin in my life and ask the Father to allow the blood of Jesus to cleanse me. Repentance activates the power of the cleansing blood of Jesus.

"In Him we have redemption through His blood, the forgiveness of sins, according to the riches of His grace." Ephesians 1:7

Just as the priest moves into the Holy Place to place the animal on the brazen altar for the sin of the Israelites, I place my sin at the mercy seat of God and ask Him to look to the Lamb of God's blood that was shed on Calvary for the forgiveness of sin.

"But Christ as High Priest of the good things to come, with the greater and more perfect tabernacle not made with hands, that is, not of this creation. Not with the blood of goats and calves, but with His own blood, He entered the Most Holy Place once for all, having obtained eternal redemption." Hebrews 9:11

Many believers make light of the power of the Blood of Jesus. It is nothing to make light of because our Savior literally went through hell to get our redemption. It is so important for the Body of Christ to not trample under our feet the precious Blood of Jesus by wallowing in unrepentant sin. The blood is our defense against any accusations of the devil, and it is only activated through true repentance. The blood of the animal that the priest would sacrifice on the brazen altar represents the Blood of the Lamb of God that was shed on the Cross for the sin of the world. It is sprinkled over the mercy seat of Heaven.

"Then he shall kill the goat of the sin offering, which is for the people, bring its blood inside the veil, do with that blood as he did with the blood of the bull, and sprinkle it on the mercy seat and before the mercy seat." Leviticus 16:15

This blood is still speaking on our behalf as we need God's judgement of mercy and grace daily.

Behind the Veil (Intimacy)

The Holy of Holies represents a place of total intimacy. This place of intimacy is a place of privilege that every born-again believer has been given. We have the right to access the Holy Father through the Blood of Jesus. Sadly, many believers never take advantage of the opportunity to commune with the Almighty God. To commune with God means to have uninterrupted worship and dialogue with God. In this time of communion, you speak to God about the content of your heart and listen for Him to tell you some of the things on His heart. As believers, we need to understand that our Father longs to fellowship with His children. He also longs for His children to listen to Him. As we consistently come into this holy place of intimacy with no other intent than to sit with God, He will begin to reveal Himself more and more to us. He will also begin to reveal yourself to you and all that He has planned for your life. As a new believer, I would always come to God with my hand out asking for my needs to be met or for blessings. As I grew a little, I would move to praying for others more. As I matured, I would set aside special time outside of my requests just to be in fellowship with Him. Don't get me wrong, there is absolutely nothing wrong with asking God for your needs to be met and praying for the needs of others. We should be totally comfortable with pouring our hearts out to our Father. We shouldn't approach God as if He isn't aware of the contents of our hearts. We should always come to Him with humility and not try and hide things in us just to look good. The Bible tells us to come to Him, make our requests known, and He will give us the desires of our heart.

Start

"Delight Thyself Also in the Lord and He Shall Give Thee the Desires of Thine Heart." Psalm 37:4

"Therefore I say unto you, What things soever ye desire, when ye pray, believe that ye receive them, and ye shall have them." Mark 11:24

"I exhort therefore, that, first of all, supplications, prayers, intercessions, and giving of thanks, be made for all men." 1 Timothy 2:1 2

We must learn to separate ourselves in the presence of the Lord to talk intimately with Him on a daily basis. As we make sitting with Him a privileged priority, we will learn the voice of God and discern His presence. Our spiritual senses will become awakened even to the point where we will no longer be able to tolerate any unrighteous behavior in our lives. Knowing the voice of God is so important. We are living in unprecedented times, and we need to discern how the Lord speaks to us. We can only accomplish this by sitting with Him in the Holy Place of

His presence uninterrupted, secluded, and with full attention on Him. Jesus exhibited a phenomenal example of running into a secluded place to fellowship and sit with the Holy Father.

"But Jesus Himself would often slip away to the wilderness and pray [in seclusion]." Luke 5:16

"In those days Jesus went out to the mountain to pray, and He spent the night in prayer to God." Luke 6:12

One night, in the wee hours of the morning as I was sleeping, I heard the Lord whisper to me, "Come sit with me". My heart smiles every time I think of that moment. Needless to say, I scurried out of bed like an excited little girl who had just gotten an invitation from her daddy to sit on his lap. As I reached to the spot where I would often meet Him, my only words upon entering was, "Yes, my Lord." Worship followed and then I'd listen for Him to speak. These times of close intimate fellowship is when He would begin to reveal to me things that were coming to the Earth. I never went to that place to ask Him for insight into world events. I just wanted to sit with my Father. I believe that because I was found faithful to sit with Him, He began to share His secrets with me. What an honor! This is exactly what happened to Abraham, Moses, Joseph, Daniel, and many more seekers of God in the Bible.

"And the LORD said, "Shall I hide from Abraham what I am doing." Genesis 18:17

"Surely the Lord GOD does nothing, Unless He reveals His secret to His servants the prophets." Amos 3:7

"But there is a God in heaven who reveals secrets…" Daniel 2:28

"The LORD confides in those who fear him; he makes his covenant known to them." Psalm 25:14, NIV

There are so many benefits to going behind the veil and learning of His Holiness. We are the new holy tabernacles of God. Our bodies are the temple of the Holy Ghost. We can use the model of the priestly responsibilities of the tabernacle to enter into a time of powerful and effective prayer. I hope I have whet your appetite to go deeper into the various types of prayer that are outlined in the chapters ahead. Apply these principles and your prayer life will never be the same.

Compare your prayer time with the priestly protocol from the Old Testament. Write down any adjustments you can make to improve your intimacy with the Lord.

CHAPTER 2

APPROACHING GOD

I like to tell a story of two brothers who I'll refer to as *James* and *John*. They lived in different cities many miles apart and could not visit often. James decided it was time to visit John and meet the new addition to their family, his nephew Jaden. Jaden was a toddler and James would be meeting him for the very first time. James was ecstatic about spending time with his nephew; however, once he arrived at John's home, to James's disappointment, Jaden was hesitant about coming to him. James was prepared to share with his nephew the love he had been dreaming about giving him once they met in person, only to be saddened by the fact that Jaden wasn't comfortable enough to freely come to him. Once Jaden spent more time around James during his visit, he became more and more comfortable with James. Jaden eventually opened up to receive the love and many gifts from his uncle James.

I have met many believers who treat God as Jaden treated his uncle James. Although James and Jaden were relatives, there was no real relationship or fellowship. Because Christians don't take the time to get to know God as Father and friend, they are hesitant to come to Him in prayer and worship. I especially notice individuals in public corporate

.10 are obviously uncomfortable with opening up to the Father
.ng His love to come upon them. His presence can be all around
.nctuary, yet they stand gazing at others' interactions with the Lord.

Our Father is bursting with great anticipation for His children to
come to Him. He has so much love to give, and this love is unfading,
boundless, and incomprehensible. He longs for us to come to Him, yet
He will never force us to come to Him. There are many scriptures in the
Bible where our Holy Father is welcoming us to come to Him and seek
His face. There are so many benefits to coming to the Father. Worship
and sitting with the Lord is wonderful prayer.

*"When You said, "Seek My face," My heart said to You, "Your face,
Lord, I will seek." Psalm 27:8*

*"Then you will call upon Me and go and pray to Me, and I will listen to
you. And you will seek Me and find Me, when you search for Me with
all your heart. I will be found by you, says the LORD." Jeremiah
29:1215*

*"He who dwells in the secret place of the Most High. Shall abide under
the shadow of the Almighty. 2 I will say of the Lord, "He is my refuge
and my fortress; My God, in Him I will trust." Psalm 91*

"Seek the LORD, and his strength: seek his face evermore." Psalm 105:4

Condemnation is one of the greatest hesitations of believers
approaching God in prayer and worship. It is only the trick of the enemy
to get believers to believe that God is mad at them for past sins. The devil
knows that if he can keep people in shame and in condemnation that
they won't approach God for forgiveness. Even if they ask the Lord for
forgiveness, people who struggle with condemnation still have a hard

time receiving forgiveness. Even if they receive God's forgiveness, they still have a hard time forgiving themselves. It is important to get to know the character and nature of our Father. We learn about His character and nature through His Word and by spending time with Him daily. When we know the truth of who the Father is, the evil one won't be able to keep us in shame and condemnation. We will begin to approach the Father freely and joyfully. Meditate on the encouraging scriptures below to overcome shame and condemnation, as well as to help you know the Father's true character and nature through the Word:

Start

"If we confess our sins, he is faithful and just to forgive us our sins, and to cleanse us from all unrighteousness." 1 John 1:9

"There is therefore now no condemnation to them which are in Christ Jesus, who walk not after the flesh, but after the Spirit." Romans 8:1

"Who shall separate us from the love of Christ? Shall tribulation, or distress, or persecution, or famine, or nakedness, or peril, or sword? As it is written: "For Your sake we are killed all day long; We are accounted as sheep for the slaughter." Yet in all these things we are more than conquerors through Him who loved us. For I am persuaded that neither death nor life, nor angels nor principalities nor powers, nor things present nor things to come, nor height nor depth, nor any other created thing, shall be able to separate us from the love of God which is in Christ Jesus our Lord." Romans 8:35-39

"For God did not send His Son into the world to condemn the world, but that the world through Him might be saved." John 3:17

"Whenever our hearts make us feel guilty and remind us of our failures, we know that God is much greater and more merciful than our conscience, and he knows everything there is to know about us.21 My

lly loved friends, when our hearts don't condemn us, we have a freedom to speak face-to-face with God." 1John 3:20-21, TPT

I, yes I, am the One and Only, who completely erases your sins, never to be seen again. I will not remember them again. Freely I do this because of who I am!" Isaiah 43:23

Access Through The Blood of Jesus

The Blood of Jesus is what cleanses us from all unrighteousness. In the Old Testament, the high priest would take the blood of bulls, goats, and lambs and annually presents them on the mercy seat in the tabernacle for the forgiveness of sin on behalf of the Israelites. Our Lord Jesus Christ gave His life and blood in order for us to gain access to the Father, fulfilling the old covenant practice once and for all.

"But Christ came as High Priest of the good things to come, with the greater and more perfect tabernacle not made with hands, that is, not of this creation. Not with the blood of goats and calves, but with His own blood He entered the Most Holy Place once for all, having obtained eternal redemption." Hebrews 9:11-12

The Blood of Jesus has many other powerful benefits such as redemption, protection, and defense against evil attacks from the enemy. But for the sake of our topic, it has afforded us the privilege to become children of God and have access to the Almighty. We should plead the Blood of Jesus over our lives daily and every time we enter into the courts of Heaven. It is what keeps our enemy at bay, and it is activated through repentance. (Hebrews 9:22) Use the Blood of Jesus to gain access to the Father anytime and anywhere!

"But now in Christ Jesus you who once were far off have been brought near by the blood of Christ." Ephesians 2:13

"Therefore, brethren, having boldness to enter the Holiest by the blood of Jesus." Hebrews 10:19

"In Him we have redemption through His blood, the forgiveness of sins, according to the riches of His grace." Ephesians 1:7

Access Through The Name of Jesus

"And now, because we are united to Christ, we both have equal and direct access in the realm of the Holy Spirit to come before the Father!" Ephesians 2:18

In John 14:6, Jesus stated, "I am the way, the truth and the life. No one comes to the Father except through me." Through Him, access has been granted to us! He gave His blood. He even gave us His name not only to pray to the Father, but also to bind anything that would try to hinder us in any way. We have been given the power of attorney. When someone gives you the power to make decisions on their behalf, it's called *power of attorney*. Jesus has given us power of attorney. We have the power to pray as if it is Him praying. We have the power over every evil spirit just like He does. He has given us that same power and authority to operate in, so that we can dominate on the Earth and be the victorious ones as He is. Not everyone has this power and authority. Only God's beloved children have the right to this. You must be in Christ to access this type of power and authority. When we pray in that wonderful and most powerful name of Jesus, all of Heaven and hell is at attention and has to respond as if Jesus Himself is praying. It's the most powerful name to ever be uttered and we, as believers, have total access to utilize it to move Heaven, Earth, and things beneath the Earth. Jesus paid the ultimate price to get this type of power and authority in His name. He did what had never been done before and what no one else could ever do. He defied death. He overthrew the powers of hell. He took the keys to the gates that lead to eternal death. He triumphed over the devil and all of His evil cohorts. In doing so, He earned the right to have the most powerful name in the world. At His name, every knee will bow, and every tongue will have to confess of His Lordship.

The authority of the name of Jesus causes every knee to bow in reverence! Everything and everyone will one day submit to this name—in the heavenly realm, in the earthly realm, and in the demonic realm. And every tongue will proclaim in every language: "Jesus Christ is Lord Yahweh," bringing glory and honor to God, His Father!

We must have a revelation of the power of the name of Jesus. It gives us access to pray to the Father directly to ask for prayers and petitions to be granted on our behalf and on the behalf of those we are praying for.

"For here is eternal truth: When that time comes you won't need to ask me for anything, but instead you will go directly to the Father and ask him for anything you desire and he will give it to you, because of your relationship with me. Until now you've not been bold enough to ask the Father for a single thing in my name, but now you can ask, and keep on asking him! And you can be sure that you'll receive what you ask for, and your joy will have no limits!" John 16:23-24, TPT

May we utilize the power, authority, access, and weapon that the name of Jesus affords us, so that we may experience a fruitful prayer life.

Seeking His Hand VS Seeing His Face

Can you imagine being in a relationship with someone who only called you when they needed something from you? I can definitely understand how that would make you feel. My husband and I have been blessed with some amazing friends. Many have been our friends for over twenty years. There are those who call us just because they are thinking of how we are doing and to see what's happening in our life. On the other hand, we have friends who call us only when they need advice, wisdom, a shoulder to cry on or to just simply vent. These would be considered those who seek our hand. Because we are mature believers, we are never offended about them only calling when they need help because we understand how to discern certain relationships. We understand that our friendship has evolved from just being friends into us mostly ministering to and being a light and example to them. We love both the seekers of our face and seekers of our hands all the same. In the same sense, there are believers who only come to the Father to ask Him for things. They don't go beyond that point and have no real *face time* with Him. This is how the children of Israel behaved. They were very content with letting Moses go and get in the face with God.

> *"The people trembled with fear when they heard the thunder and the trumpet and saw the lightning and the smoke coming from the mountain. They stood a long way off and said to Moses, "If you speak to us, we will listen. But don't let God speak to us, or we will die!" "Don't be afraid!" Moses replied. "God has come only to test you, so that by obeying him you won't sin." But when Moses went near the thick cloud where God was, the people stayed a long way off." Exodus 20:19-20*

Because they didn't take the time to know the Holy Father, they became fearful to come to Him. Moses knew the Holy Father enough to understand that there was love and care within His thunderous voice that came from the mountain. Our Father desires us to seek His face more than we seek His hand. It is for our benefit more than our Lord's. There are so many precious things that come from seeking the face of the almighty God.

"He made known His ways to Moses, His acts to the children of Israel."
Psalm 103:7

True enough, the Lord desires to show us His hand by answering our prayers, but there is so much more when we seek His face. He will reveal His character and nature to us Himself, thus giving us a lasting impression and encounter with our mighty Savior. This reminds me of the time when I got an invitation from the Almighty Himself to come and sit with Him.

Soaking In His Presence

Oftentimes, my husband and I will just sit and hold hands while enjoying each other's presence. There may not be much conversation, but we are soaking up the love between the two of us without saying many words other than exchanging an *I love you* here and there. This could go on for several minutes while I lay back on his chest. We simply enjoy each other's presence in that way. Believe it or not, the Lord desires this type of intimacy with His children in the holiest way. He is such a vast and self-sustaining God and yet He desires personal time with His children. When the Lord began calling me to come and sit with Him, I was astounded that He would be so mindful of me. I knew He loved me and that He wanted me to seek Him, but it touched me in a new way when I heard Him say to me "Come sit with me." In sitting with the Lord in prayer, He will begin to speak to you about things you would never have asked about. He will begin to reveal His ways and secrets to you. Based on my experience, this will begin to happen when there is trust established and a consistent time that you show up to meet Him. When He can trust you with His secrets, He will begin to open up more realms and revelations to you. All from simply coming to sit with Him to seek His face and not His hand. These times in the secret place will birth a level of intercession within you. Mostly because of some of the content that He shows you. You will begin to want to stand in the gap for things and people on the Earth. Let's go a little deeper in the birthing of an intercessor in this next chapter.

Imagine yourself sitting on the lap of Almighty God. Practice pouring your heart out to Him in a way that is unfiltered and filled with humility. Write down the content of your heart here. Make this a daily habit for the rest of your life. Remember, content in your heart changes, so be true to the Spirit of Truth.

CHAPTER 3

SOAKING TO INTERCESSION

One stormy night in the mid-nineties, I was sitting in the living room of our home in the rocking lazy boy. I can remember very vividly lightning strikes and sounds of thunder while rain fell for hours. There were sirens and flash flood warnings going off on television and outside. I suddenly felt this strong urgency to pray in the Spirit. It was a deep grieving in my spirit, and I had no idea what was going on in the Spirit. I just knew I needed to pray and not let up. I prayed for what seemed like hours in my heavenly language as it was impossible for my mind to comprehend or articulate what my spirit was sensing. I knew that there was some type of battle going on in the Spirit realm, but I had no other details as to what this battle was concerning. After praying hard and fervently for a good while, I finally got a release to start praising and thanking the Lord. Not long afterwards, I got a phone call telling me what the time of intercession I had just encountered was all about. It turns out that a relative of mine was in the battle of their life. They were apparently outside in the storm and had collapsed in the street. It was reported that the flood waters had risen on the street where they collapsed, and that they were in danger of drowning. Someone in the neighborhood got word to our family and they were able to rescue my relative and save their life. It was not a coincidence that all of this was happening at the time I got an alert in my spirit to start praying. I am so grateful that I was sensitive enough to yield myself over to the Spirit of Intercession because it saved a life that stormy night.

Have you ever suddenly felt a strong urgency to pray for something you had no idea about? If so, then that was the Spirit of Intercession looking for a yielded vessel to pray the will of the Father in the Earth. One thing about the Spirit of Intercession is that it can hit you at any moment and time. You can be in the middle of a deep sleep, doing household chores, driving, washing your hair, or simply watching television, when it hits you. There are no time restraints when the Spirit of Intercession can hit you because the Spirit of God is always looking for vessels whom He can show Himself strong through, just as much as the enemy is always on the prowl to kill, steal, or destroy. Intercessors are needed on the clock for every prayer watch. Let's look a little deeper into what true intercession really is.

What is Intercession?

Simply put, intercession is standing in the gap on behalf of a person, place, or thing through prayer. Although that's a simple definition, intercession is not to be taken for granted as it is very important and much needed. It can literally save lives just as it saved my relative's life as I yielded to it. Our Father is looking for more vessels to stand in the gap on behalf of others.

> "So I sought for a man among them who would make a wall, and stand in the gap before Me on behalf of the land, that I should not destroy it; but I found no one." Ezekiel 22:30

Intercession does not always have to be initiated by our Father, and we should not just wait for His prompting in order to intercede. I am a firm believer of being led by Holy Spirit in all that we do. You don't have to wait to be led by Holy Spirit to pray. You should, however, be led by Holy Spirit on what to pray for. Prayer, in and of itself, is never wrong. It's what you pray that can get you in trouble, at times. I will share more on that in the chapter on *The Courts of Heaven.*

Jesus stated in Luke 18:1, "... men ought always to pray and not to faint." Apostle Paul also stated that we should pray without ceasing in 1 Thessalonians 5:17. Our hearts should always be postured in a position of prayer, whether we feel called to be an intercessor or not.

My First Experience Interceding

Back in the early nineties, I had a dream about a plane that exploded in the sky over a deep blue ocean in the middle of the night. I specifically remember the feeling of this woman who I saw fall into the ocean from being ejected from the plane's explosion. As I saw her plummeting towards the bottom of the ocean, I felt everything she was feeling. I felt her fear, loneliness, hopelessness, and despair as she continued to sink and yet she was still alive. I woke up carrying all of those emotions from the dream although I had no idea who this person was, when this event happened, or was going to happen. Nor did I know if indeed things would turn out tragically for this young woman. All I knew within myself was that I must pray for this situation. I could not shake the dream for several weeks. Every time I closed my eyes, I would see her sinking in the dark black ocean. I couldn't pray for anything else for several weeks other than to intercede for the lady in the dream. When I blessed my food, I saw her sinking. When I tried to pray for my kids, I saw her sinking.

When I prayed at church, I saw her sinking. It became obvious that I needed to pray through this dream until I got a release. Many believers don't know what it means to pray through. To pray through means to pray in the Spirit every chance you get about a situation and to not stop until there is a release in your spirit that it is finished. I prayed through this dream until one night, I dreamed that I saw this same woman crawling from the ocean to the shore as she had survived the fall into the ocean. I woke up and I felt the peace to move on to other things in prayer. From that day on, I stopped seeing her sinking when I closed my eyes. One day when my husband and I were watching the news, we saw a breaking news report that a plane had crashed over a body of water and there were no survivors except one woman. My heart leaped and I immediately told my husband that I believe that is who I was praying and interceding for. I didn't consider myself to be an intercessor at the time, but I was indeed operating in the function of an intercessor, as I yielded to the Spirit of Intercession.

You don't have to know all of the details of a situation in order to intercede for the perfect will of God for a situation. By praying in the Spirit, which is in a heavenly language, you are praying *perfect prayer* to the Father. Holy Spirit is the great Helper who helps us as we yield our tongues to Him. You will learn more about this in chapter seven.

"Likewise the Spirit also helps in our weaknesses. For we do not know what we should pray for as we ought, but the Spirit Himself makes intercession for us with groanings which cannot be uttered. Now He who searches the hearts knows what the mind of the Spirit is, because He makes intercession for the saints according to the will of God. And we know that all things work together for good to those who love God, to those who are the called according to His purpose." Romans 8:26

"For he who speaks in a tongue does not speak to men but to God, for no one understands him; however, in the spirit he speaks mysteries." 1 Corinthians 14:2

Because our understanding, or intellect, is limited, we need insight and assistance from Holy Spirit to help us to pray effectively.

"......the effective, fervent prayer of a righteous man avails much." James 5:16

The Amplified translations says:

".....The earnest (heartfelt, continued) prayer of a righteous man makes tremendous power available [dynamic in its working]."

Our heartfelt intercession on behalf of others who are in need makes tremendous power available to them and causes dynamic change in their situations. My commitment to pray through the known and unknown caused a life and destiny to be spared from being cut short. Your commitment to do the same is needed. The more intercessors the greater the impact and the better our world around us will be. We have the power and authority to change lives, destinies, and our world! The woke Church is the most powerful entity in the Earth as we have all of Heaven working on our behalf, assisting us in carrying out the will of God. Notice, I said the "woke Church," and not the sleeping Church. We must be awake and sensitive to hear the Spirit of God. We must be alert in order to move at His command. As the days become shorter and evil becomes more aggressive, we, as the praying Church, must stand on our watch to see what the Lord would have us say, declare, pray, and do to enforce the Kingdom of our God. A woke Church is a watching Church.

Jesus, Our Constant Intercessor

Everyone needs an intercessor. Whether a person is saved or unsaved, good, or evil, rich, or poor, all are in need of an intercessor. Our Redeemer is interceding for us constantly. He is our High Priest who is before the Father, day in and day out, standing in the gap on our behalf. He has shielded us from countless dangers, seen and unseen. We are in the Body of Christ because of His faithful intercession on our behalf. When we miss the mark, He is there to intercede for us.

"Who is he who condemns? It is Christ who died, and furthermore is also risen, who is even at the right hand of God, who also makes intercession for us." Romans 8:34

"Therefore He is also able to save to the uttermost those who come to God through Him, since He always lives to make intercession for them." Hebrews 7:25

"My little children, these things I write to you, so that you may not sin. And if anyone sins, we have an Advocate with the Father, Jesus Christ the righteous." 1 John 2:1

Although we have a Chief Intercessor in Jesus, that doesn't relieve us of our responsibility to intercede for one another. Our prayers and supplication can make the difference in life-or-death situations. When the Apostle Peter's life was on the line, the saints gathered together to make intercession on his behalf. The disciple's prayers caused the Holy Father to move on Peter's behalf. He assigned Peter an angel of deliverance who performed a miracle for him to escape jail and death.

"Peter was therefore kept in prison, but constant prayer was offered to God for him by the church. And when Herod was about to bring him

out, that night Peter was sleeping, bound with two chains between two soldiers; and the guards before the door were keeping the prison. Now behold, an angel of the Lord stood by him, and a light shone in the prison; and he struck Peter on the side and raised him up, saying, "Arise quickly!" And his chains fell off his hands. Then the angel said to him, "Gird yourself and tie on your sandals"; and so he did. And he said to him, "Put on your garment and follow me." So he went out and followed him, and did not know that what was done by the angel was real, but thought he was seeing a vision. When they were past the first and the second guard posts, they came to the iron gate that leads to the city, which opened to them of its own accord; and they went out and went down one street, and immediately the angel departed from him.

And when Peter had come to himself, he said, "Now I know for certain that the Lord has sent His angel, and has delivered me from the hand of Herod and from all the expectation of the Jewish people." So, when he had considered this, he came to the house of Mary, the mother of John whose surname was Mark, where many were gathered together praying. And as Peter knocked at the door of the gate, a girl named Rhoda came to answer. When she recognized Peter's voice, because of her gladness she did not open the gate, but ran in and announced that Peter stood before the gate. But they said to her, "You are beside yourself!" Yet she kept insisting that it was so. So they said, "It is his angel."

Now Peter continued knocking; and when they opened the door and saw him, they were astonished. But motioning to them with his hand to keep silent, he declared to them how the Lord had brought him out of the prison. And he said, "Go, tell these things to James and to the brethren."

And he departed and went to another place." Acts 12:5-17

Watchmen

As I would go into my secret place to sit with the Lord, I would often fall into a watchmen's posture. My spirit would be saying, "Yes, Lord." I knew when things would shift from a worshipping time to a watching mentality. The best way I can explain it is to imagine being in a dark cave that you're unfamiliar with. Your senses are extremely heightened to try and figure out what you can see, feel, smell, or hear. Even though your eyes are seeing black, they are working really hard to make out any images, doors, stumbling blocks, sounds, etc. That's how it is when I step into watching in the Spirit. My spirit man is looking to see what can be picked up on the spiritual radar. I begin to operate in strong discernment and start picking up people, conversations, matters in people's heart, and even certain events that will come upon the Earth.

In the Bible days, cities would be fortified with great walls to keep the people within safe, and keep the enemy out. They would establish watchmen upon the walls to not only see what was entering the city, but to also warn everyone when the threat of an enemy was approaching.

"I have set watchmen on your walls, O Jerusalem; they shall never hold their peace day or night. You who make mention of the Lord, do not keep silent, and give him no rest til He establishes and til He makes Jerusalem a praise in the earth." Isaiah 62: 6-7

On November 13, 2013, as I found myself watching in the Spirit, I heard these words, "Over 200 million Americans will be affected by a turn of events in the Earth." I had no idea what that meant, but I knew it was something of great importance. I needed to be praying into this turn of events, and I sensed I needed to continuously cry out for God to have mercy on us Americans. At the time of this writing, we are in the midst of a worldwide pandemic. The COVID-19 virus has not only affected 200 plus million Americans, but has had global impact on our world. I received that spiritual intel seven years prior to it manifesting. I have been praying for mercy for seven years and although we have seen many tragic deaths, I believe it could be much worse had there not been prayer into it before it hit the Earth. It is important to watch as well as pray. As I said before, we must get beyond praying for us four and no more. We need every believer to be mature in their prayer life, so that we can cut off the plan of the enemy to kill, steal, and destroy. As kingdom intercessors, it is imperative that we are ahead of what is coming to the Earth. We must also go to our own company of leaders and intercessors to pray over what we are shown, as one can chase a thousand, but two can put ten thousand to flight. We must warn when danger is coming as led by Holy Spirit.

"Son of man, I have made you a watchman for the house of Israel; therefore hear a word from My mouth, and give them warning from Me." Ezekiel 3:17

It's important as an intercessor to know who and when to tell what God reveals to you when watching in the Spirit. Not everyone was mature enough to hear what I saw concerning an event that would affect two hundred million people in America. For an immature believer, this information could strike fear in them, causing them to live a disturbed life. Our Lord is not into creating fear in others. We should use wisdom when sharing revelations we get from the Lord. Nevertheless, there are some things we see that we are not meant to carry alone. In such cases, I highly recommend you have a person or group that is mature enough to help carry that prayer assignment.

"For thus has the Lord said to me: "Go, set a watchman, Let him declare what he sees." Isaiah 21:6

Sleeping Watchmen

What is the point of setting a watchman only to find out that he has been sleeping on the job? Who knows what came in and out of the city???

"His watchmen are blind, They are all ignorant; They are all dumb dogs, They cannot bark; Sleeping, lying down, loving to slumber." Isaiah 57:10

I can remember early in my salvation being awakened in the early morning to pray. This was before I knew I was called to be an intercessor. I must admit that I would feel irritated when my sleep was interrupted. Unfortunately, I wanted my sleep more than I wanted to talk to the Lord, or potentially save a life. I would just complain within and wonder, why am I up? Then, I would roll over and go right back to sleep. This would happen regularly until I received a prophetic word that God was calling me to get up and pray during the night watch. I cannot say that I was ecstatic about losing sleep, but I knew lives were at stake. I didn't want to be like the leaders being described in Isaiah 57:10; a watchman who is blind, ignorant, dumb dogs that can't bark, lying down and loving slumber. In context, the Prophet Isaiah was describing leaders who were tasked with watching for the people of God. They were doing everything but what they were called to do. As intercessors, we must posture ourselves to see, know, educate, warn, and watch in the Spirit. Don't despise the fact that you will have to sacrifice sleep. Trust me, the reward of the testimonies of life-altering victories that come as a result of your sacrifice far outweigh the comfort of sleep.

Watchmen Who See

As intercessors, the Lord will allow us to see specific people to pray for. Meaning, He will allow you to literally see their faces in the Spirit. I have seen faces of people that I knew personally, and I had no doubt that I needed to intercede for them. I have seen faces of famous people in which I was assigned to intercede on their behalf for a season. One day, while watching in the Spirit, I saw the face of this very famous female rap star. The Lord gave me insight into her life and specifically asked me to pray for her salvation. I prayed for her for at least a year or so. As an intercessor, you must be sensitive as to when your prayer assignment is complete. If you stop praying too soon, the enemy could bring tragedy at any moment. Years after my assignment was up for interceding for the rap star, I saw a documentary on her life. In the documentary, she shared how she was raised in the Church but strayed away from the Lord and became very depressed in the music world. She talked about the demonic pull on her life that left her feeling hopeless. Miraculously, she escaped that dark world. After many years of living that fast life, she recommitted her life to the Lord. I honestly believe it was because she had an intercessor assigned to her life who did not quit in the middle of the assignment.

Unlawful Prayers

As I was praying for the rap star, I was only praying what I was told to pray for, which was for her salvation. Intercessors get into deep trouble by praying from their own intellect or desires. This is very dangerous and could cause some spiritual backlash to come upon them. Praying only from your intellect concerning a situation can lead to unlawful prayers. One day as my husband and I were flying back from a trip, I heard the

Lord speak to me about an intercessor. He told me that this intercessor was experiencing attacks on their body because they had been praying unlawful prayers. I had never heard the term *unlawful prayers* before in my life. I asked the Lord what it meant.

Unlawful Prayers: praying your own will and desires as opposed to praying the known, or revealed, will of God. Praying what you'd rather see happen, making it a controlling prayer, which is witchcraft.

He explained to me that unlawful prayers are when a person is praying for something that they desire to happen in another person's life against the will of the person they are praying for. It's not Spirit-led prayer. It's really a self-motivated prayer and it can get you into a lot of trouble. For instance, one of my family members was involved in a relationship that did not look like anything Godly. They were pleased with the relationship, but I knew it was pulling my family member away from God. I began to pray that the Lord would break them up, remove that person who was pulling them away from God, and let that person break it off with my family member, etc., etc., etc. The Lord corrected me and told me what I should have been praying. I should have been praying for their souls to be saved, but I was too caught up in wanting to see them broken up. Those were unlawful prayers.

Pray only the revealed will of God for people. If you don't know the revealed will of God for people you're interceding for, then just pray in the Spirit for them. Usually, when you focus on them while praying in the Spirit, Holy Spirit will reveal more to you to pray and declare over the person or situation.

Prayer Watches, What's Yours?

Do you wake up at the same time many nights of the week? Chances are that's your assigned prayer watch. The Bible speaks of various prayer watches, or times of prayer. Cindy Jacobs, in her book, "Possessing the Gates of the Enemy," gives her definition of prayer watches as "intense, concentrated prayer for a specific time or purpose." She states, "The Jewish people prayed every three hours, at nine a.m., noon, and three p.m. They taught that Abraham instituted the first watch, Isaac the second, and Jacob the last." There are a total of eight prayer watches in a day that covers a twenty-four-hour period. They are broken up into four-night watches and four-day watches.

Night Watches
1st watch 6pm-9pm
2nd watch 9pm-midnight
3rd watch 12am-3am
4th watch 3am-6am
Day Watches
5th watch 6am-9am
6th watch 9am-12 noon
7th watch 12pm-3pm
8th watch 3pm-6pm

Over the years, I have learned that my primary watch to pray and intercede is in the 4th watch of the day (3am-6am). It doesn't necessarily mean that's the only time that I pray, but that is the most consistent time that I feel God awakens me to watch, pray, or sit with Him. As an intercessor, it is important to understand that a consistent prayer time is key to maturing into a prophetic intercessor. Establish a prayer watch and stay with it until the Lord says change, keeping in mind that it won't be your only time to pray. It's your definite committed time of prayer.

Prophetic Intercession

In 2014, we planted a church in a region about a hundred miles south of our home church in Memphis, TN. We and our church intercessors were praying intensely for that region. One day as we were in prayer for it, I saw a vision concerning the region. I saw, in the Spirit, a bulldog chained to the top of the tallest building in that city. It was at attention on all four legs looking out over the region. It was as if it was strategically placed there to see what was coming in or out of the city. It was sort of like a watchman, but it was a principality assigned to that region. As I prayed more into that vision, it was revealed to me that this was a religious principality who was set up to block the authentic move of God over that region. I alerted the intercessors of the vision, and we all began to pray fervently to gain more insight from the Lord of exactly what we were up against. The Lord began to speak to me more and revealed that this region had been cursed by someone who sold his soul to the devil for personal riches, and it opened the door for poverty to overtake the land. The area is popular for folklore and witchcraft. The religious spirit was very strong in the churches. The true power of God would hit in a revival from an outsider, but it could never be sustained by the local Pastors. This revelation and insight is what happens when you tap into prophetic intercession. The Lord allows you to get spiritual insight into a situation you're praying about in order for you to speak, declare, and prophesy change.

Prophetic intercession is when revelatory information is given by the Spirit of the Lord when interceding for a person or situation. This is information that you couldn't possibly know by your own personal intellect. I can recall countless testimonies where our intercessors received insight into areas that helped bring breakthroughs in the Spirit realm that manifested swiftly in the natural. One evening, we received an alert in our intercessors group that a relative of a member of the church was missing and suicidal. Everyone began urgently praying for the relative as we knew time was of great essence. This person needed to be found quickly to prevent them from doing any harm to themself. One of the intercessors began seeing snap shots of their specific location. This prophetic information from the Spirit allowed the authorities to locate the relative unharmed. This is prophetic intercession.

Prophetic intercession does not only have to happen just because a request was made. Many times, God will initiate us to pray prophetically. It takes the discipline of getting control of your mind and really being in tuned with your spirit to hear or see what prayers are needed and for who.

The late Reinhard Bonnke tells a story on a video posted to the Official Reinhard Bonnke Facebook Page of a time when he learned the power of intercession as a young man. As he was on a mission field in Africa, he became very thirsty on an extremely hot day. He chose to drink water from a well not knowing that the water was polluted. Shortly afterwards, he became deathly ill. He was so sick that he began hallucinating. He saw death trying its best to take him as he was on his sick bed for several days. Suddenly, he heard a voice of someone praying for him. He realized it was a voice of a woman who was a member of his father's church back in Germany. The morning after he heard her prayers in the Spirit, his fever broke, and he began to slowly recover. After his full recovery, he inquired back home of the woman praying for him to see what prompted her to do so. She responded that the Lord woke her up in the middle of the night and told her to get up and intercede for Reinhard because he is dying in Africa. She prayed until she broke through and got a peaceful release. Because of her obedience and diligence, Reinhard Bonnke lived a long fruitful life as he won millions of souls to the Lord during his time in ministry. His destiny was not cut short because of a prophetic intercessor. Prophetic intercession is a powerful gift that every believer can and should be sensitive enough to operate in.

Prophets should be intercessors just as much as intercessors should pray prophetically. Because these gifts are in direct communication with the Father, they will often flow interchangeably. I will never understand a Prophet who doesn't like to pray. The Bible has many examples of Prophets praying and interceding for people and nations. In my opinion, something is really off with a person who says they are a Prophet and do not like to pray. We must expect to pray effectively, prophetically, and powerfully as intercessors.

I want to remind you that every born-again believer can operate in intercession, as well as prophetic intercession. You don't have to be marvelously gifted, called to the fivefold ministry offices, or be a leader in any capacity to pray. All the Lord is looking for is yielded vessels willing to tap into the heart of our Father through worshipful prayers. He is looking to do great exploits through saints who are hungry to see the perfect will of God in people's lives.

Take this opportunity to commit to yielding yourself to hear when the Lord calls you into a time of intercession. Write your commitment here and refer to it often to remind yourself that you will yield to the Spirit of Intercession.

CHAPTER 4

BIBLICAL PRAYERS
OF INTERCESSION

Our Lord is looking for someone to work with Him in preserving His purpose for mankind. The fact that the almighty, all-knowing, all-powerful God wants to work with man is amazing. The reality is that God needs us to enforce His will. That's right! God needs you and me. We are His representatives on the Earth. We have been given dominion over the Earth. We have the power to effect change and we do this by partnering in prayer with our Father. Prayer is an invitation for the Lord to get involved with the affairs of man. We need the Lord's involvement to see the change needed in the hearts of man, and especially in pressing circumstances. It is the Lord's desire that we experience Heaven on Earth. Earth can be a living hell if believers don't stand in their authority to push back the plans of the enemy. We must take by force the perfect will of God as our adversary won't just sit back without any opposition towards us. He hates anything that looks like the Kingdom of God. Although the Kingdom of God suffers violence, the violent take it by force! (Matthew 11:12) Let's look at some mighty people on the Earth that partnered with God in intercession for mankind.

Abraham's Prayer of Intercession

Intercessors have great compassion. That compassion moves them to go before our Father regardless of the inconvenience, i.e. loss of sleep, pressing deadlines, or busyness of life. The compassion for people and their souls compels us to get up in the wee hours of the morning to get before the Father.

Abraham showed his compassion even to those who practiced wickedness in the land of Sodom and Gomorrah. In Genesis chapter eighteen, Abraham learns of the plan of God to destroy the people in the cities of Sodom and Gomorrah. He is moved with compassion for them and stands in the presence of the Lord to plead for mercy on their behalf. He even went as far as bargaining with the Lord. Although Abraham lost the bargain, it showed his compassion for mankind.

> *"Then the men turned away from there and went toward Sodom, but Abraham still stood before the Lord. And Abraham came near and said, "Would You also destroy the righteous with the wicked? Suppose there were fifty righteous within the city; would You also destroy the place and not spare it for the fifty righteous that were in it? Far be it from You to do such a thing as this, to slay the righteous with the wicked, so that the righteous should be as the wicked; far be it from You! Shall not the Judge of all the earth do right?" So the Lord said, "If I find in Sodom fifty righteous within the city, then I will spare all the place for their sakes." Genesis 18:22-26*

When you're interceding for people or situations, don't stop until you hear the Lord say that the judgement is final. I remember a time when I received a bad report of a family member who died prematurely. I jumped up and began to head to the scene ready to pray for a miracle. I was determined for God to raise them up from their death bed until I heard Holy Spirit say to me, "No, it is final!" My heart was broken but I knew that if I went to pray for them, I would be praying against the will of God. To do so is very dangerous. Always pray and never stop interceding unless you get the release that the judgement is final.

Moses' Constant Intercession

Moses saved the Israelites from the wrath of Almighty God several times with his intercession. The Bible describes the Israelites as a rebellious and stiffnecked people who often returned to their roots of Egyptian idolatry.

> *"And the LORD said to Moses, "I have seen this people, and indeed it is a stiff-necked people! Now therefore, let Me alone, that My wrath may burn hot against them, and I may consume them. And I will make of you a great nation." Then Moses pleaded with the LORD his God, and said: "LORD, why does Your wrath burn hot against Your people whom You have brought out of the land of Egypt with great power and with a mighty hand? Why should the Egyptians speak, and say, 'He brought them out to harm them, to kill them in the mountains, and to consume them from the face of the earth'? Turn from Your fierce wrath, and relent from this harm to Your people. Remember Abraham, Isaac, and Israel, Your servants, to whom You swore by Your own self, and said to them, 'I will multiply your descendants as the stars of heaven; and all this land that I have spoken of I give to your descendants, and they shall inherit it forever.'" So the LORD relented from the harm which He said He would do to His people." Exodus 32:9-14, NKJV*

If you're interceding for a rebellious person, don't let up. Reason with the Lord just as Moses did concerning their purpose being fulfilled for His Name's sake!

"So He said He would destroy them--had not Moses His chosen one stood before Him in the breach to divert His wrath from destroying them." Psalm 106:23

Nehemiah's Intercession

Not only did Nehemiah serve closely with the King, but he was also an intercessor who knew how to fast and get a prayer through to our Father. We need bold intercessors who work closely with political leaders and powers. More often than not, believers who are placed in places of great influence such as Nehemiah become silent, forget about their purpose for being in that position, and succumb to selfpreservation. Even Esther had to be reminded by her uncle Mordecai that she had been placed in a position of power and influence for such a time as that. Nehemiah heard about the needs of his people back home and went to the Lord in prayer and intercession. He knew that his people had brought upon themselves their own reproach and he prayed and repented on their behalf.

Just as Nehemiah repented on behalf of the nation, we must do the same for our nation and the people we are interceding for, so that the Lord will wipe away the ordinance of sin against them.

"And I said: "I pray, Lord God of heaven, O great and awesome God, You who keep Your covenant and mercy with those who love You and observe Your commandments, please let Your ear be attentive and Your eyes open, that You may hear the prayer of Your servant which I pray

before You now, day and night, for the children of Israel Your servants, and confess the sins of the children of Israel which we have sinned against You. Both my father's house and I have sinned. We have acted very corruptly against You, and have not kept the commandments, the statutes, nor the ordinances which You commanded Your servant Moses. Remember, I pray, the word that You commanded Your servant Moses, saying, 'If you are unfaithful, I will scatter you among the nations; but if you return to Me, and keep My commandments and do them, though some of you were cast out to the farthest part of the heavens, yet I will gather them from there, and bring them to the place which I have chosen as a dwelling for My name. Now these are Your servants and Your people, whom You have redeemed by Your great power, and by Your strong hand. O Lord, I pray, please let Your ear be attentive to the prayer of Your servant, and to the prayer of Your servants who desire to fear Your name; and let Your servant prosper this day, I pray, and grant him mercy in the sight of this man." For I was the king's cupbearer."
Nehemiah 1:5-11

Not only did Nehemiah pray, he also was not afraid to ask the King for what he needed in order to help his people. He fasted, he prayed, he asked the King for the resources needed, and he went to help build the wall. Those who have been placed in positions of influence, please be reminded that not only can your prayers change outcomes for the people you serve, but your action is also needed as well. Be led by the Lord on what He may instruct you to say or do after you pray.

Job Intercedes for His Friends

One of my closest friends and I lost touch for several years. Our lifestyles became vastly different when I gave my life to Christ. I would often wake up in the middle of the night with her heavily on my heart. I didn't have a phone number to reach her to see what was going on with her, so all I could do was pray for mercy, protection, and her salvation. Since then we have reconnected. She told me stories of how her life was in danger many times during our time apart as she was living a very fast life in the streets. I had no idea! All I knew was she needed my prayers. She has since committed her life to Christ, and we talk regularly. I believe it was intercession that saved her life the many times she was in danger. Everyone, even our close friends, need our prayers and times of intercession.

> *"The Lord said to Eliphaz: What my servant Job has said about me is true, but I am angry at you and your two friends for not telling the truth. So I want you to go over to Job and offer seven bulls and seven goats on an altar as a sacrifice to please me. After this, Job will pray, and I will agree not to punish you for your foolishness. Eliphaz, Bildad, and Zophar obeyed the Lord, and he answered Job's prayer." Job 42:7-9, CEV*

Ezekiel's Intercession

Ezekiel witnessed firsthand God's judgment against the Israelites. What he witnessed caused him to fall to his knees and cry out to the Lord for answers in intercession.

> *"After that, I heard the Lord shout, "Come to Jerusalem, you men chosen to destroy the city. And bring your weapons!" I saw six men come through the north gate of the temple, each one holding a deadly weapon. A seventh man dressed in a linen robe was with them, and he was carrying things to write with. The men went into the temple and stood by the bronze altar. The brightness of God's glory then left its place above*

the statues of the winged creatures inside the temple and moved to the entrance. The Lord said to the man in the linen robe, "Walk through the city of Jerusalem and mark the forehead of anyone who is truly upset and sad about the disgusting things that are being done here." He turned to the other six men and said, "Follow him and put to death everyone who doesn't have a mark on their forehead. Show no mercy or pity! Kill men and women, parents, and children. Begin here at my temple and be sure not to harm those who are marked." The men immediately killed the leaders who were standing there. Then the Lord said, "Pollute the temple by piling the dead bodies in the courtyards. Now get busy!" They left and started killing the people of Jerusalem.

I was then alone, so I bowed down and cried out to the Lord, "Why are you doing this? Are you so angry at the people of Jerusalem that everyone must die?" The Lord answered, "The people of Israel and Judah have done horrible things. Their country is filled with murderers, and Jerusalem itself is filled with violence. They think that I have deserted them, and that I can't see what they are doing. And so I will not have pity on them or forgive them. They will be punished for what they have done." Just then, the man in the linen robe returned and said, "I have done what you commanded." Ezekiel 9:1-11

There are times when our intercession will be impotent. When the Lord has deemed that all grace has been lifted from someone or a situation, we as intercessors must step back and watch what is imminent. I have witnessed judgment fall on individuals who chose to walk in a season of sin too long. The sin ranged from speaking negatively about men and women of God, to sexual promiscuity, to rebellion, etc., which led to sickness or even death. As intercessors, we must be careful not to allow our own hearts to become bitter or hardened because our intercession didn't turn the situation or the person. Our intercession cannot go against anyone's personal will to not repent. The people who the Lord judges are people who become callous to the Lord's conviction and are not horrified at sin as seen in Ezekiel 9. This was even in the Church (temple). The leaders of the Church were the first ones that were killed because they were found without the mark of God on them.

Daniel's Intercession

After learning of the prophetic decree that Jerusalem would lie in ruins for seventy years, Daniel began to fast and pray for his nation. He repented for his sin and for the sin of his forefathers. As a result of his intercession, the Lord revealed specific timelines concerning the current judgement of his people.

> *"I am your servant, Lord God, and I beg you to answer my prayers and bring honor to yourself by having pity on your temple that lies in ruins. Please show mercy to your chosen city, not because we deserve it, but because of your great kindness. Forgive us! Hurry and do something, not only for your city and your chosen people, but to bring honor to yourself. I was still confessing my sins and those of all Israel to the Lord my God, and I was praying for the good of his holy mountain, when Gabriel suddenly came flying in at the time of the evening sacrifice." Daniel 9:17-19*

Daniel's intercession caused the Lord to release the Holy Angels to manifest answers. We will talk more about angelic assistance in a later chapter as they are pertinent to intercessors.

Joel's Instructions to the Priest to Intercede

If we are going to see the glory of God over our land, then we must be intentional about interceding for it. We are the supernatural change agents in the Earth. If we don't continue to pray for our land, then it will surely become an impoverished embarrassment. Our Father wants to bless our land because we, His children, are inhabitants of it.

> *"Tell my servants, the priests, to cry inside the temple and to offer this prayer near the altar: "Save your people, Lord God! Don't let foreign nations make jokes about us. Don't let them laugh and ask, 'Where is your God?'" The Lord Will Bless the Land. The Lord was deeply concerned about his land and had pity on his people. In answer to their prayers he said, "I will give you enough grain, wine, and olive oil to satisfy your needs. No longer will I let you be insulted by the nations."*
> *Joel 2:17*

What example of biblical intercession can you relate to the most? Write how you would respond in prayer to interceding for your family, friends, ministry, and nation.

CHAPTER 5

UTILIZING THE COURTSOF HEAVEN

There are so many facets to prayer. There is prayer of worship, prayer of intercession, prayer in tongues, and also another form of intercessory prayer in the *Courts of Heaven*. Praying in the Courts of Heaven is when you appear before the Courts of Heaven to ask for a specific judgement from God on behalf of yourself or another. Heaven has a real courtroom! God is the Righteous Judge on the Throne. In going before the Courts of Heaven, you must approach the Righteous Judge differently than you would in a general prayer. You must be aware of specific information before you approach the throne just as an attorney must present specific information in order to convince a natural judge to rule in their favor. You must also be right with God yourself before attempting to appear before the courts lest an accusation is made against you while you're there. Below are scriptures where the Holy Father is referred to as Judge in the courts.

"O Lord, You have pleaded the case for my soul; You have redeemed my life Lord, You have seen how I am wronged; Judge my case." Lamentations 3:58-59, NKJV

"But, O Lord of hosts, You who judge righteously, Testing the mind and the heart, Let me see Your vengeance on them, For to You I have revealed my cause." Jeremiah 11:20, NKJV

"God is a just judge, And God is angry with the wicked every day."

Psalm 7:11, NKJV

"I watched till thrones were put in place, And the Ancient of Days was seated; His garment was white as snow, And the hair of His head was like pure wool. His throne was a fiery flame, Its wheels a burning fire; A fiery stream issued and came forth from before Him. A thousand thousands ministered to Him; Ten thousand times ten thousand stood before Him. The Court was seated, And the books were opened." Daniel 7:9-10, NKJV

God is a holy Father and a righteous Judge. His judgments are in line with who He is, which is Truth. He is also full of grace and mercy. He desires for His children to be acquitted of every charge against them. That's why He allowed Jesus to be slain before the very foundation of the world. (Revelation 13:8) He knew we would need saving from our sin and He made sure He made a way out for us through our Lord Jesus.

Jesus is our advocate in the Courts of Heaven just like a defense attorney would defend you if you had a case against you. Attorneys are paid a lot of money to defend their clients; however, every case they defend does not always get acquitted. Our heavenly defense attorney presents the most powerful evidence ever in presenting His Blood to the Father, which gives us total clemency for all of our debt of sin, if we apply it over our lives. He is our advocate, our intercessor, our scapegoat, our deliverer!

"And the Lord said, "Simon, Simon! Indeed, Satan has asked for you, that he may sift you as wheat. But I have prayed for you, that your faith should not fail; and when you have returned to Me, strengthen your brethren." Luke 22:31-32, NKJV

"My little children, these things I write to you, so that you may not sin. And if anyone sins, we have an Advocate with the Father, Jesus Christ the righteous." I John 2:1, NKJV

"Who is he who condemns? It is Christ who died, and furthermore is also risen, who is even at the right hand of God, who also makes intercession for us." Romans 8:34, NKJV

The Holy Father gave the only begotten Son, so that He could demonstrate who He is to mankind and shed His blood for the remission of our sin. Without the shedding of blood, there is no remission or forgiveness of sin. (Hebrews 9:22) Jesus' blood is sprinkled over the mercy seat in Heaven and it is speaking around the clock on our behalf, exclaiming that there is a sacrifice for our stay of judgment. (Hebrews 12:24) So, as you petition the Courts of Heaven, arm yourself with this truth. Repent of your sin and plead the Blood of Jesus over yourself. Bring your case, or the case of who or what you're interceding for, and reason with the mighty, merciful Judge.

"Come now, and let us reason together," Says the Lord, "Though your sins are like scarlet, They shall be as white as snow; Though they are red like crimson, They shall be as wool." Isaiah 1:18, NKJV

To *reason* means to talk it over. To *talk it over* means to have a dialogue with who you're speaking with. We must dialogue with the Lord about what we are requesting. State your petition, wait, and listen to hear what response, or verdict, the Lord renders. Plead your cause utilizing the Blood of Jesus as your primary witness for the pardon you need.

Satan is the accuser of the brethren. He is always going around seeking how he can accuse us before God in the Courts of Heaven. It is vitally important that you not show up in the Courts of Heaven praying unlawfully. Enter with the Blood of Jesus over your life through repentance from all of your sin. Repent on behalf of anyone you're bringing before the courts for any sin they may have committed. Ask the Father if the current judgement is final. If not, proceed to plead for a judgement of grace and mercy. Satan is very crafty in that he knows he has to have a legal right to petition the court or just as in a natural court, it could be thrown out. Satan accuses us so that he can get a judgement against us. He would love for the Lord to remove the hedge of protection from us, so he can cut our lives short of fulfilling purpose.

> *"Now there was a day when the sons of God came to present themselves before the Lord, and Satan also came among them. And the Lord said to Satan, "From where do you come?" So Satan answered the Lord and said, "From going to and fro on the earth, and from walking back and forth on it." Then the Lord said to Satan, "Have you considered My servant Job, that there is none like him on the earth, a blameless and upright man, one who fears God and shuns evil?" So Satan answered the Lord and said, "Does Job fear God for nothing? Have You not made a hedge around him, around his household, and around all that he has on every side? You have blessed the work of his hands, and his possessions have increased in the land. But now, stretch out Your hand and touch all that he has, and he will surely curse You to Your face!" And the Lord said to Satan, "Behold, all that he has is in your power; only do not lay a hand on his person." So Satan went out from the presence of the Lord."* Job 1:6-12, NKJV

"Then I heard a loud voice saying in heaven, "Now salvation, and strength, and the kingdom of our God, and the power of His Christ have come, for the accuser of our brethren, who accused them before our God day and night, has been cast down. And they overcame him by the blood of the Lamb and by the word of their testimony, and they did not love their lives to the death." Revelation 12:10-11, NKJV

When you are faced with situations that won't move, it's possible that you need to appear before the Righteous Judge and plead your case. Some circumstances take more than just a declaration or scripture quote. When you have done all manner of praying and when nothing seems to change, it would be good to check with the Righteous Judge to see if there are any accusations before Him from the accuser of the brethren. It's a good practice to always ask three questions when facing turbulent times for an extended season:

- Is this the consequence of my wrong actions?
- Is God trying to teach me something?
- Is this the enemy attacking me?

Either way, it's always good to repent of all sin and generational iniquity from your bloodline. Plead the Blood of Jesus over yourself and go before the Righteous Judge to ask for a judgement of grace and mercy for yourself or whoever it is that you're praying for. There have been many times I've gone before the Courts of Heaven on behalf of church members who were in desperate need of a judgement of divine grace and mercy. I've seen many be raised from their bed of affliction. I have even pleaded for my own cause when I'd been so sick that it felt like death was lurking at my door. I pled my cause before the Righteous Judge, and He gave me a judgement of grace and mercy. I was healed within twenty-four hours. Things will move when repentance has cleaned your slate and there's no longer a cause for the evil one. You will no longer be a lawful captive of the terrible.

"But thus says the Lord: "Even the captives of the mighty shall be taken away, And the prey of the terrible be delivered; For I will contend with him who contends with you, And I will save your children." Isaiah 49:25, NKJV

Write out your prayer before entering the Courts of Heaven. Write out your prayer while in the Courts of Heaven on behalf of your community, city, nation, family member, or yourself.

CHAPTER 6

PRAYING IN ALIGNMENT WITH GOD'S HEART

Have you ever wondered if it was right for you to be praying for certain things? I can remember a time, as a baby believer, when I felt I needed to know that I was praying according to the will of God. I would often wonder, "How do I know if I'm praying rightful prayers?" Not being sure that I was praying the right prayers certainly made me uncertain that my prayers would be answered. I wanted to be sure God was hearing me and that He would answer me. In this chapter, I will share three ways of praying in alignment with God's heart in order to pray effectively. Remember, effective prayers mean answered prayers.

Sonship

The first way you know you're praying in alignment with God's heart is when you're praying from the place of sonship. When I speak of *sonship*, I am speaking of the spiritual position that has been given to all born-again believers. This is a genderless position in that it's spiritual. The Apostle Paul stated, "There is neither Jew nor Gentile, neither slave nor free, nor is there male or female, for you are all one in Christ."

(Galatians 3:28) Naturally speaking, we are sons and daughters of the Most High God. Spiritually, we are sons and heirs of the Most High God. We have been seated together with Christ in heavenly places. We are joint heirs with Christ which makes Him not only our Lord and Savior, but our elder brother! Many believers don't see themselves as a son. Therefore, they don't pray as sons. When we don't have a revelation of our sonship, we won't be confident enough to pray and believe that our prayers will be answered. A revelation of sonship brings another level of confidence. Not confidence in ourselves, but confidence in our Father. On the contrary, not having a revelation of your sonship will cause low self-esteem, low self-worth, and a life of unfulfilled needs and desires. Below are scriptures validating who we are to our Father.

> *"But as many as received him, to them gave he power to become the sons of God, even to them that believe on his name." John 1:12, KJV*

> *"For you did not receive the spirit of bondage again to fear, but you received the Spirit of adoption by whom we cry out, "Abba, Father." The Spirit Himself bears witness with our spirit that we are children of God, and if children, then heirs—heirs of God and joint heirs with Christ, if indeed we suffer with Him, that we may also be glorified together." Romans 8:15-17*

> *"Behold what manner of love the Father has bestowed on us, that we should be called children of God! Therefore the world does not know us, because it did not know Him." 1 John 3:1*

What good father would not want to give his child everything that he knows is good for him? If natural fathers know how to give everything good that their child asks of them, how much more our Heavenly Father gives us our heart's desire.

"If you then, being evil, know how to give good gifts to your children, how much more will your Father who is in heaven give good things to those who ask Him!" Matthew 7:11, NKJV

Having a renewed mind of sonship is indicative of getting your prayers answered. The Lord is not pleased with viewing yourself in any other way. He that comes to God must believe that He is and that He is a rewarder of those who diligently seek Him. (Hebrews 11:6) We must believe that He is our Father, and we are sons and joint heirs.

One day, I was studying the scriptures in Daniel 10:11. It reads: "And he said to me, "O Daniel, man greatly beloved, understand the words that I speak to you, and stand upright, for I have now been sent to you." While he was speaking this word to me, I stood trembling." When I read this, I started praying to the Lord telling him how much I wanted to be like Daniel who the angel called a man greatly beloved. I looked at other translations to see exactly what beloved meant. *Beloved* was also translated as well respected, honored, highly esteemed, and loved. In the middle of me telling the Lord how much I wanted to be like Daniel, loved, well respected, honored and highly esteemed, the Lord said to me, "What makes you think you're not!" I was shocked! Up until that point, I had not realized that I was thinking like an orphan and not from sonship. I operated in an orphan spirit and didn't know I was hindering myself and my prayers. An orphan spirit will have you oblivious to what you can have in your Father's house and have you going without when provision is there. A case in point is the brother of the prodigal son in Luke 15. The oldest brother was very upset that his father was celebrating his brother who had finally come back home after taking his sonship and inheritance for granted.

"But he was angry and would not go in. Therefore his father came out and pleaded with him. So he answered and said to his father, 'Lo, these many years I have been serving you; I never transgressed your commandment at any time; and yet you never gave me a young goat, that I might make merry with my friends. But as soon as this son of yours came, who has devoured your livelihood with harlots, you killed the fatted calf for him.' "And he said to him, 'Son, you are always with me, and all that I have is yours." Luke 15:28-31, NKJV

The oldest brother had everything that the father had in his possession and yet he acted as if he wasn't a son. It wasn't until his younger brother was celebrated and given all the best that he felt less appreciated. We can't allow envy and jealousy to enter our hearts when we see our other brothers and sisters who have a revelation of their sonship get their prayers answered. We all have the same rights and privileges but it's the children who have a revelation of their sonship that will get the manifestations and benefits of that revelation. Answered prayers are certainly a benefit of sonship!

It's your personal revelation of your sonship that will develop your personal prayer life. Many are praying in alignment with who taught them to pray, i.e. sounding like their teacher and addressing The Father the same way. When you get your own bond with your Heavenly Father and pray out of the revelation of sonship, you begin to develop your own personal sound in prayer.

Jesus was so confident with His sonship, He confirmed in the ears of His followers that His Father always heard Him when He prayed.

"Then they took away the stone from the place where the dead man was lying. And Jesus lifted up His eyes and said, "Father, I thank You that

You have heard Me. And I know that You always hear Me, but because of the people who are standing by I said this, that they may believe that You sent Me." John 11:41-42, NKJV

Below are five important points to remember concerning praying from your sonship:

1. Sonship functions out of love and acceptance. We have been accepted into the beloved because of the blood of our Lord and Savior Jesus Christ. He will never reject anyone who comes to Him in repentance and humility. You must know that He will never reject you in order to come boldly before His throne to ask for mercy, grace, and anything else you need. You are always accepted and never rejected!

2. If you don't have a revelation of sonship, you won't have confidence to ask for anything in prayer.

3. Sonship comes with an inheritance. When you're aware of your inheritance, you will ask for what you need and desire.

4. When you don't see yourself how God sees you, you won't have the faith to even ask for certain things, or believe you can have certain things.

5. When you don't have a revelation of your sonship, you operate in an orphan spirit, and you won't /can't pray in alignment with God's heart.

Jesus is the only begotten Son, but not the only son. He was the only son fathered by God. But we have become sons by His blood and therefore we have access, relationship, and fellowship as sons of God. We have rights and privileges just like Jesus. We have been seated in heavenly places in Christ. We have been adopted as sons. Your prayers being answered or not answered is directly related to the revelation of your sonship.

Priestship

The second way of praying in alignment with God's heart is to pray from your *priestship* position. The high priest went before the Holies of Holies to bring sacrifices for the sins of the nation of Israel. This was a type and shadow that our High Priest, Jesus the Righteous, was to bring His blood before the Holy Father as a sacrifice for our sin once and for all. Because of the holy sacrifice that Jesus made, we now have a priestly anointing to go before our Father on behalf of others, including all people, governments, nations, etc. in prayer. We bring ourselves to Him as spiritual sacrifices to do His will. To intercede, to petition, to plead for mercy along with our holy worship and lifestyle.

> *"Coming to Him as a living stone, rejected indeed by men, but chosen by God and precious, you also, as living stones, are being built up a spiritual house, a holy priesthood, to offer up spiritual sacrifices acceptable to God through Jesus Christ." 1 Peter 2:5*

Here are three things to remember about praying from your position of priestship:

- We are called to minister to the Holy Father through worship. The Levite priesthood were set apart as a holy lineage and would be called upon to go before the warriors in battle on several occasions. They led the way in battle with shouts of praise and worship with many victories as a result. (2 Chronicles 20:21)

- We are called to offer spiritual sacrifices to the Lord. This includes praise and prayer to name a few. Intercession is a form of spiritual sacrifice. When we choose to take time out of our regular schedule to intercede for those in need, it's considered a spiritual sacrifice. (Hebrews 12:15)

- We are called to walk upright before the Lord. Just as the Levite priesthood was set apart as the righteous and to cleanse themselves of anything unholy, we are expected to do the same as a holy priesthood by and through the Blood of Jesus. If they approached the Holy Father and had not done the proper ceremonial cleansing, it could have cost them their lives.

When we approach the Holy Father from our priestship position, we bring Him the spiritual sacrifices that He will in no wise turn away. He welcomes our worship and prayers of intercession.

Kingship

The third way of praying in alignment of God's heart is to pray from your *kingship* position. To pray from your divine kingship position is to know your authority and the dominion that has been given to you as a born-again believer. A King has a domain and has authority within that domain. Our Father has given us authority and dominion. We have been given authority to rule and reign in the Earth.

"Now when He had taken the scroll, the four living creatures and the twenty-four elders fell down before the Lamb, each having a harp, and golden bowls full of incense, which are the prayers of the saints. And they sang a new song, saying: "You are worthy to take the scroll, And to open its seals; For You were slain, And have redeemed us to God by Your

blood Out of every tribe and tongue and people and nation, And have made us kings and priests to our God; And we shall reign on the earth." Revelation 5:8-10

As a king and priest unto our God, we have the power to declare and decree. Once a king makes a decree, it becomes law, and it can't be reversed by anyone. Not even the king who made the decree can reverse his decree. As believers, we must renew our minds to know that we have been granted kingship. We are not just children of God. We are royalty. We have the power to speak into existence what we need, and it must manifest according to our words. Our Father is so awesome that He gave us sonship, the ability to come to Him in our priestship and the power and authority to decree in the atmosphere anything we need that is according to His Word and His Will.

"You will also declare a thing, And it will be established for you; So light will shine on your ways." Job 22:28

"So Jesus answered and said to them, "Have faith in God. For assuredly, I say to you, whoever says to this mountain, 'Be removed and be cast into the sea,' and does not doubt in his heart, but believes that those things he says will be done, he will have whatever he says. Therefore I say to you, whatever things you ask when you pray, believe that you receive them, and you will have them." Mark 11:22-24, NKJV

Here are four important things to remember about operating in your kingship.

1. You must change your mental posture to reflect your kingly position. As your mind goes, so does your body. As a man thinks, so is he. You will never rise above what is in your soul. You must think like a king in order to operate as a king.

2. In the kingly position, you have authority and dominion. You must rise up and take authority over anything and everything that does not line up with what the Word says about your situation.

3. You should make kingly decrees according to the Word of Truth. Open your mouth up and start decreeing. Praying silently is fine for conversation. There will come a time when you need to stand up in your kingly authority and make decrees. The very world we live in now was framed by the Word of God. God said let there be light, and light was!

4. Your decrees are never spoken at God but always spoken to your circumstances. You may always petition with God, reason with God, but you never decree at God. You may remind Him of what His Word says but even that is not realistic because He is His Word, and He already knows what His Word says. What we are really saying is, "God, we know what we are standing on and that is Your living Word.

What if things don't move? Keep speaking. Keep declaring. Keep listening. What are you listening for? To make sure that you and God are still saying the same thing. Keep saying the same thing He is saying, and your prayers will manifest in due season.

Examples of Kingly Declarations

I declare that I am hungry for your Word of Truth. That I walk in truth always. Never will I be deceived. I have the Spirit of Truth and He leads and guides me into all truth. Your truth is my shield and buckler.

I declare that I hear You clearly. My spiritual ears are open to Your instructions. I have an ear to hear what the Spirit of the Lord has to say to me as His Church. My spiritual ears are in tune with Heaven's agenda.

Because I am in tune with Heaven, I will never live in lack. I declare that I will always live in abundance. Provision is my portion. In every area of my life! The young lions may lack and suffer hunger, but they that seek the Lord will not lack anything. (Psalm 34:10) I'm a seeker of the Lord. I seek first the Kingdom of Heaven and His righteousness, and I declare that good things will be added to me!

I declare that doors of supernatural grace are open to me. I declare that I experience unusual success in every area of my life. I declare Psalm 1 over my life, "Blessed is the man who walks not in the counsel of the ungodly, nor stands in the path of sinners, nor sits in the seat of the scornful; But his delight is in the law of the LORD, And in His law he meditates day and night. He shall be like a tree planted by the rivers of water, that brings forth its fruit in its season, Whose leaf also shall not wither; And whatever he does shall prosper."

I declare that things are changing for the better for me right now! I speak forth my increase, I speak forth my healing, I speak forth my deliverance. I declare change for the better!

I speak to the dry bones as your prophet Ezekiel did and I command every dry place to be watered, to come to life, to begin to move, Ezra 37

"Now this is the confidence that we have in Him, that if we ask anything according to His will, He hears us. And if we know that He hears us, whatever we ask, we know that we have the petitions that we have asked of Him." 1John 5:14

When you pray the Word of God as applicable to your situation, you don't have to have any doubt because the Holy Father is *one* with His Word. He cannot be separated from His Word.

"In the beginning was the Word, and the Word was with God, and the Word was God." St. John 1:1

The Lord is always ready to perform His Word. He said that He would hasten to perform His Word. That word *hasten* means that God is willing and ready at any time to make His Word come to pass.

"Then said the LORD unto me, Thou hast well seen: for I will hasten my word to perform it." Jeremiah 1:12, KJV

You don't have to worry if the Lord wants to perform His Word in your life. He honors His Word and He promised that His Word would never return to Him void.

"For as the rain comes down, and the snow from heaven, And do not return there, But water the earth, And make it bring forth and bud, That it may give seed to the sower And bread to the eater, So shall My word be that goes forth from My mouth; It shall not return to Me void, But it shall accomplish what I please, And it shall prosper in the thing for which I sent it." Isaiah 55:10-11, NKJV

The Word is His will. So, when you pray His Word, you pray His will. He will perform His Word with signs following.

"And they went out and preached everywhere, the Lord working with them and confirming the word through the accompanying signs. Amen." Mark 16:20, NKJV

From your kingship position, write out decrees that you want to see come to pass for yourself or others.

CHAPTER 7

PRAYING IN THE SPIRIT

My husband was in South Africa back in 2008 on a mission trip with a church group from our city. There were many nights that I could not sleep while he was away. It wasn't the usual I can't sleep because I missed my husband being next to me. This was different and strong. I was being prompted to pray in the Spirit every night. Back then, I could not just pick up a cell phone and call him on his. I had no idea what was happening, but I knew it was something serious. The strong urgency in my spirit in the middle of the night kept me up. I had no words to pray in my native language because I had no details of anything that was happening. Although I was very concerned, I didn't feel helpless because I had the Holy Spirit on the inside. He was the one alerting me that I needed to pray in my heavenly language (praying in tongues). Praying in tongues, or in the Spirit, is speaking to God in a divinely inspired language that comes from my spirit. It's a language that I did not learn but it was given to me when I received the Gift of the Holy Ghost with the evidence of speaking in other tongues. Once my husband returned, I could not wait to ask him all about his adventures in Africa. I gained so much insight as he told me of the many dangerous situations they were in. One incident in particular was when they were traveling back to the living quarters near sunset when all of a sudden, torrential rain fell on them for several minutes. Because of the excess water on the gravel roads they were traveling on, the jeep became stuck in the mud. Now mind you, this is in the middle of the safari close to getting dark! We know all too well that the wild hunts at night. Sure enough, a lioness walked behind the vehicle within a couple of feet. By the grace of God and the prayers at night, the lioness did them no harm. They were also in situations where hyenas were approaching them, and no one was harmed. There were many other serious events that occurred, but everyone came back safe and untouched. There is no natural way I could have known what my husband and the mission group were encountering. But praying in the Spirit is all I knew to do. I felt it from the core of my belly to pray fervently and without ceasing until a peace came over me. This is what you call praying through. When prompted by the Holy Spirit that something is wrong, you must pray until you get a release to stop and until you get a peace in your spirit. When you don't know what you are to pray for, having a heavenly language to go to can be the difference between life and death.

> *"Likewise the Spirit also helps in our weaknesses. For we do not know what we should pray for as we ought, but the Spirit Himself makes intercession for us with groanings which cannot be uttered. Now He who searches the hearts knows what the mind of the Spirit is, because He makes intercession for the saints according to the will of God." Romans 8:26-27, NKJV*

If you are a person who endeavors to pray effectively, you would definitely benefit from praying in other tongues. We are very limited in our prayers when we only pray from our intellect. We don't know everything. Holy Spirit knows everything. If you have ever gone to God in prayer but you ran out of words to say and left prayer frustrated and even more uncertain, then you need the Baptism of the Holy Ghost with the evidence of speaking in other tongues. Can you pray Spirit-led prayers without speaking in tongues? Sure you can. But praying in the Spirit allows you to enter into another realm of powerful prayer in the Spirit. Many believers have taken on the mindset that them being born again is more than enough for them. However, Luke specifically stated that Jesus was coming and that He would baptize us with the Holy Ghost and with fire.

> *"John answered, saying to all, "I indeed baptize you with water; but One mightier than I is coming, whose sandal strap I am not worthy to loose. He will baptize you with the Holy Spirit and fire." Luke 3:16, NKJV*

Jesus specifically told the disciples to wait for Holy Spirit to come on them and when He came upon them, they would receive dynamite power! Why leave anything on the table that is highly recommended by the Lord Himself.

> *"… for John truly baptized with water, but you shall be baptized with the Holy Spirit not many days from now." Acts 1:5, NKJV*

> *"But you shall receive power when the Holy Spirit has come upon you; and you shall be witnesses to Me in Jerusalem, and in all Judea and Samaria, and to the end of the earth." Acts 1:8, NKJV*

I can't begin to tell you of all of the many different experiences I've had with Holy Spirit helping me to pray out things I had no idea about. There have been many instances where I've sensed a strong urgency to pray for my children. I can remember praying for one of my daughters who was in a rebellious teenage state at the time. I felt a sudden urgency to intercede for her by praying in the Spirit. I just had a *knowing* that I needed to pray for my daughter. It was a knowing from the inside and not from outside information. I can remember sitting in my chair in my bedroom rocking and speaking in other tongues for so long that I lost track of time. Then it happened, a sudden peace came over me. Then, I sensed I should just stop and begin to thank and praise the Lord. I later found out why I was interceding so hard for her. It wasn't long afterwards that we received a call that she was in an altercation. The other individuals came with a knife to kill my daughter. They slashed her car tires, but she came away without a scratch on her. I know that I would never have had the intellect to pray for my daughter as I needed. The power of praying in other tongues gave me the ability to intercede and caused deliverance to come to my child. Every believer needs the power of the Holy Ghost to pray in other tongues!

I am always praying for my children. I plead the Blood of Jesus over them regularly. But there are special times when you know the Lord is impressing upon your heart to intercede for them. There was another time when Holy Spirit impressed strongly upon my heart to intercede for my other daughter. I knew she was in some kind of danger that would be detrimental to her. This time, I was led to call my husband and our other daughter together, so we could meet in her room to pray and intercede together. I didn't know why He led me to involve them this time. But I do know the Scripture says "one can chase a thousand and two can put ten thousand to flight" with the Lord as our helper. (Deuteronomy 32:30) We immediately went into the Spirit realm praying in our heavenly language. We prayed, decreed, and declared her safety and deliverance until peace came upon us. Well, the prayers reached Heaven! A couple of months later, she was involved in a head-on car collision that left her with a broken bone and a few minor injuries. This accident was meant to kill her. The person who hit her was going at a deadly rate of speed and did not hit the brakes even upon impact. It was a horrible scene. Thankfully, everyone survived. It was definitely the prayers of the righteous and praying in the Spirit that helped us pray through to victory for my daughter.

Having the ability to pray in the Spirit takes all limitations off of your prayer life. It's impossible to pray effectively for hours from your intellect without having the facts to pull from. But when you can pray in the Spirit, you don't need all of the facts. Holy Spirit has all of the facts because He is all knowing. He will pray perfectly through you as you yield. Another benefit of having the ability to pray in other tongues is that it edifies and builds your spirit up. When you're low spiritually, begin to pray in tongues and you will feel your fire become rekindled in your spirit.

If you do not have the ability to pray in other tongues and you are interested in learning more so that you can receive, for the sake of staying on course, I have listed some scriptures for you to study. When you have the faith to receive, just ask Holy Spirit to come and fill you and He will.

- Romans 8:26
- 1 Corinthians 14: 2
- 1 Corinthians 14:14-15
- Acts 1-4
- Luke 11:9-13

Take a moment to pray in the Spirit. Ask for the interpretation of what you just prayed. Write down what you hear.

CHAPTER 8

ANGELIC ASSISTANCE

In1996, I was pregnant with my youngest daughter. It was in my last trimester when my husband was called to go out to the West Coast to pray and lead his dying cousin to the Lord. That year, many airplanes were crashing, and it brought much concern to me. Not only was I concerned about my husband's safety, but I was really worried about him not being home in time for the birth of our baby. I couldn't imagine giving birth with him not at my side. I certainly would never stand between him winning a soul to Christ, so I didn't complain outwardly. I prayed and talked to the Lord about my concerns. Let me just take a moment to say that there is nothing that you can't talk to your Heavenly Father about. Absolutely nothing! He already knows what's bothering us, but He just wants us to verbalize it to Him in our time of fellowship with Him. So, time went on and it was coming close to the date for my husband to fly out. One night, I woke up out of a deep sleep and looked over towards my husband's side of the bed and saw a huge angel who stood at least 9 feet tall. He was adorned in all white with huge broad shoulders. He was standing at attention with his sword drawn as if he dared anything to come near our bed. I instantly was led to turn around to my side of the bed and there stood another angel identical to the angel that stood at the headboard of my husband's side of the bed in the same warrior's position and his sword drawn. Amazingly, I wasn't afraid or even shocked at what I saw. I was at so much peace that I laid my head back on the pillow and continued my deep pregnancy sleep. The Lord allowed me to see in the realm of the Spirit to bring answers and comfort to me concerning the prayers I had been praying. I'm so glad that we have a God who loves to answer His children's prayers! It brought me so much relief to know that we have angels assigned to us to keep us in all of our ways.

"For He shall give His angels charge over you, To keep you in all your ways. In their hands they shall bear you up, Lest you dash your foot against a stone." Psalm 91:11-12, NKJV

Not only are they assigned to protect us, but they are also found in the scriptures carrying out the Lord's decrees, delivering divine messages, judgments, and warnings and in warfare against the enemy.

Many believers do not understand angels' roles; therefore, they don't call on the Lord, who is the Commander of Angels Armies, to ask Him to release them on their behalf. Working on our behalf is one of the reasons they were created by the Lord.

"But to which of the angels has He ever said: "Sit at My right hand, Till I make Your enemies Your footstool"? Are they not all ministering spirits sent forth to minister for those who will inherit salvation?" Hebrews 1:13-14, NKJV

Kevin Zadia wrote in his book titled, "The Agenda of Angels," how an angel appeared to him with a warning message that saved him from taking a detour off of his divine destiny. He wrote: "It was as though I was suspended above my body. I could see a large angel standing in the doorway. The door had physically opened! That was just not possible because, as I noted previously, that door was double-locked. I still was not mobilized as I watched the angel approach me. He bent down and grabbed me by the arm. He lifted me up, and I regained some of my strength. As I stood before him, I noticed his attire. From top to bottom, the angel wore a full Roman centurion's uniform. He was very tall. He may have been about nine or ten feet tall, and he perhaps weighed eight hundred pounds. He spoke with such authority as he began to address me. He said that he had come on behalf of the Most High God. He said, "I have been sent from the presence of the Most High to tell you that you must separate yourself unto God. There are individuals whom you have befriended from whom you are to separate yourself. No longer spend time with these people, for not only are they not in the will of God, but these people are about to be judged." While he was talking to me, I saw the individuals about whom he was speaking. The group consisted of a group of people about twelve in number who had befriended me. The angel started to talk to me about my calling, but then he was interrupted by the Holy Spirit. I could not hear what was being said to him by the Holy Spirit, but he held his hand up to motion for me to wait. He then told me that he was called immediately to another place. He asked me to go to the prayer room, which was down the hallway. He said that instead of his completing this message from the Most High God, the Holy Spirit would finish the message. I objected to this situation. I was impressed with the awesomeness of this angel. He was standing within three feet of me. I wanted him to continue to talk to me. I was looking at him and was studying his armor, which was very intricate and beautiful. The power that came from this being was so amazing, and it was a natural reaction for me to want him to complete his message because no one would have wanted him to leave. I felt safe because of the authority that I sensed within this angel. He walked in such godly authority, and awareness of his authority within just made me boldly confident in the protection of God. I then said to the angel, "You are already here, so please, just finish the message." At this, the angel became very stern with me, sterner than he previously had been. He said, "I said go to the prayer room, and do it now!" At this, the angel turned and pointed to the prayer room door, which was down the hallway. Then, the angel walked quickly down the hallway. As he walked away, he disappeared into thin air! Six months after this experience with the angel, those twelve or so individuals were all expelled from college for misconduct. If I had not listened to the angel's warning from that evening, I would have been implicated as being part of their group, and I also would have been expelled. The angel was sent to help me understand a situation that I could not possibly have personally foreseen at the time that the angel revealed it to me. The angel also knew completely what would happen to these individuals in the next six months. God's foreknowledge had been revealed to me, and that angel was sent to warn me."

In the previous chapter, we talked about the importance of praying in the Spirit. I want to mention here that when you pray in the Spirit, you also activate the power of God to release angelic activity on your behalf. When we pray in the Spirit, we are praying the perfect will of God. Angels help to manifest the perfect will of God.

In Chapter six, we talked about the importance of operating in your kingship and declaring the Word of the Lord to change situations and circumstances. Well, how do you think the situations and circumstances change? Right, the angels start moving on behalf of the one who makes the decrees.

"Bless the Lord, you His angels, Who excel in strength, who do His word, Heeding the voice of His word." Psalm 103:20

I have never seen in Scripture where we are to command angels to work for us; however, I have seen where Jesus said that He could ask the Holy Father to send legions of angels to work on His behalf.

"But Jesus said to him, "Put your sword in its place, for all who take the sword will perish by the sword. Or do you think that I cannot now pray to My Father, and He will provide Me with more than twelve legions of angels?" Matthew 26:52-53, NKJV

We can ask the Father to send angels on our behalf against our enemies. I'm speaking of spiritual enemies, evil spirits, not your evil neighbor. The Bible says that the weapons of our warfare are not carnal but mighty in God to pull down strongholds. (2 Corinthians 10) We don't wrestle against flesh and blood but against principalities, powers, rulers of darkness and spiritual wickedness in high places. (Ephesians 6) I can remember a time when I was praying for our city. We were experiencing demonic activity because serious crimes were beginning to rise more than usual. As I began to pray in the Spirit, the Lord showed me a vision of a huge principality over our city. This was no ordinary principality. It was so large that I couldn't measure in feet how tall it stood. It seemed as tall as the twin towers! This principality was clothed in what looked like a military general's uniform. It had many stripes on its shoulders. As soon as I made eye contact with it, I started to run to it like David ran toward Goliath to cut its head off. Before I could take off, I heard the Lord say to me, "Don't go after it, you need reinforcement." When I came out of the vision, I was bewildered. In my mind, I was thinking that I had all power and authority over all the works of the devil according to Luke 10:19. Holy Spirit constrained me because He wanted me to let Him fight this battle. He later gave me the revelation that I needed to call upon Him to release the high-ranking warring angels to deal with this principality. Spirits never get tired, but they like to wear us out, so they can overcome us. Instead of battling a principality on my own, I asked Holy Father to send those high-ranking angelic hosts to fight for me. The Lord taught me a very valuable lesson in rightly dividing the Word with personal revelation. Sure, we have power and authority over all the works of the devil, but there are battle rankings that we need to be aware of. We need to know when to call in reinforcement lest we find ourselves out ranked. Many saints call themselves *warring in the Spirit* and become spiritually fatigued. The Lord has given us a master plan and strategy to defeat the evil attacks from the devil. We are to pray to the Father in His Name about what we are dealing with. We are to use our authority to bind and loose. We are to plead the Blood of Jesus as our defense. We are to ask for angelic assistance to excel in strength on our behalf as we declare the Word of the Lord. We are to believe by faith that victory is already ours as the angelic hosts work and do the warring. This is what it means when the scripture says, the battle is not yours, but the Lord's. He releases His angels to fight for us. Let's look at scriptures where the angels fought for the people of God.

"It happened after this that the people of Moab with the people of Ammon, and others with them besides the Ammonites, came to battle against Jehoshaphat. Then some came and told Jehoshaphat, saying, "A great multitude is coming against you from beyond the sea, from Syria; and they are in Haz Azon Tamar" (which is En Gedi). And Jehoshaphat feared, and set himself to seek the Lord, and proclaimed a fast throughout all Judah. So Judah gathered together to ask help from the Lord; and from all the cities of Judah they came to seek the Lord." 2 Chronicles 20

Here we see the enemy rise up to come against the children of God. The people of God sanctified themselves to a fast and sought the Lord about what they should do to overcome this pending battle. When faced with adversity, a trial, or an attack, it is vitally important to pray to the Father to receive a divine strategy on how He would have you move. Just because the Lord will be the one to bring the victory doesn't mean we won't need to hear what He is saying to us, or have a role to play. Your role may simply be to just fast, or worship, or even make some changes in your routine. It just depends on what God will instruct you to do. As the children of Judah set themselves aside to seek the Lord, the Spirit of the Lord began to speak through Jahaziel with instructions and the outcome if they obeyed.

"Then the Spirit of the Lord came upon Jahaziel the son of Zechariah, the son of Benaiah, the son of Jeiel, the son of Mattaniah, a Levite of the sons of Asaph, in the midst of the assembly. And he said, "Listen, all you of Judah and you inhabitants of Jerusalem, and you, King Jehoshaphat! Thus says the Lord to you: 'Do not be afraid nor dismayed because of this great multitude, for the battle is not yours, but God's. Tomorrow go down against them. They will surely come up by the Ascent of Ziz, and you will find them at the end of the brook before the Wilderness of Jeruel. You will not need to fight in this battle. Position yourselves, stand still and see the salvation of the Lord, who is with you, O Judah and Jerusalem!' Do not fear or be dismayed; tomorrow go out against them, for the Lord is with you." 2 Chronicles 20:14-17

They went down the next day just as the Lord had spoken. They put the praisers out front and declared that the Lord was great, and His mercy endures forever. God moved on their behalf.

"Now when they began to sing and to praise, the Lord set ambushes against the people of Ammon, Moab, and Mount Seir, who had come against Judah; and they were defeated. For the people of Ammon and Moab stood up against the inhabitants of Mount Seir to utterly kill and destroy them. And when they had made an end of the inhabitants of Seir, they helped to destroy one another." II Chronicles 20:22-23, NKJV

The Lord did the work on behalf of His people. Their enemies destroyed one another without the children of Israel ever having to lift a finger in battle. Although angels weren't mentioned in this particular passage, I do believe they had a role to play in this victory. Let's look at a scripture where angels were specifically mentioned in bringing victory in battle on behalf of God's people.

In 1 Kings 19, King Hezekiah found himself under the attack of the wicked king of Assyria. The message of Rabshakeh came into the ears of King Hezekiah, and it struck fear in him. He immediately went before the Lord in prayer and sent word to Prophet Isaiah. Can you identify with King Hezekiah? Oftentimes, the spirit of fear will attack us when we receive a bad report. As we regain our composure and focus on the One who has the capacity to deliver us, we can remain calm and allow Him to speak.

"And so it was, when King Hezekiah heard it, that he tore his clothes, covered himself with sackcloth, and went into the house of the Lord. Then he sent Eliakim, who was over the household, Shebna the scribe, and the elders of the priests, covered with sackcloth, to Isaiah the prophet, the son of Amoz. And they said to him, "Thus says Hezekiah: 'This day is a day of trouble, and rebuke, and blasphemy; for the children have come to birth, but there is no strength to bring them forth. It may be that the Lord your God will hear all the words of the Rabshakeh, whom his

master the king of Assyria has sent to reproach the living God, and will rebuke the words which the Lord your God has heard. Therefore lift up your prayer for the remnant that is left." II Kings 19:1-4, NKJV

Hezekiah was a Godly king. He knew exactly what to do when he heard the bad report. Hezekiah went to the one who had the capacity to deliver him out of the hand of his enemy. He sought the Lord. He sought the commander of the angel's army in prayer. Look at King Hezekiah's heartfelt supplication on behalf of his nation:

"And Hezekiah received the letter from the hand of the messengers, and read it; and Hezekiah went up to the house of the Lord, and spread it before the Lord. Then Hezekiah prayed before the Lord, and said: "O Lord God of Israel, the One who dwells between the cherubim, You are God, You alone, of all the kingdoms of the earth. You have made heaven and earth. Incline Your ear, O Lord, and hear; open Your eyes, O Lord, and see; and hear the words of Sennacherib, which he has sent to reproach the living God. Truly, Lord, the kings of Assyria have laid waste the nations and their lands, and have cast their gods into the fire; for they were not gods, but the work of men's hands—wood and stone. Therefore they destroyed them. Now therefore, O Lord our God, I pray, save us from his hand, that all the kingdoms of the earth may know that You are the Lord God, You alone." II Kings 19:14-19, NKJV

He answered through his Prophet Isaiah that they would see victory from this situation. When you're faced with unfathomable circumstances, wait, and see what the Lord would say. Oftentimes, we react immediately. We start scrambling for ways that we can deliver ourselves, inadvertently digging a deeper hole. The Lord desires to answer His people. He doesn't take pleasure in us being left in the dark about any situation. We are children of the light because He is our light! After the

Lord spoke the prophetic decree about Assyria's defeat, angels started moving into position to bring the Word of the Lord to pass.

"And it came to pass on a certain night that the angel of the Lord went out, and killed in the camp of the Assyrians one hundred and eighty-five thousand; and when people arose early in the morning, there were the corpses—all dead." II Kings 19:35, NKJV

The angels excelled in strength at the Word of the Lord! They battle for us, so we don't have to become spiritually fatigued. They are built for spiritual battles. We must ask the Father to utilize them to fight for us! Decree that angels are working on my behalf while I sleep, while I'm away, and when I go to and fro! The Lord fights for His people through the angelic host of Heaven.

There are so many more instances in the Bible where angels showed up as a result of the prayers of the righteous. While the disciples were in a prayer meeting on behalf of Peter who had been jailed and on death row, an angel showed up in the middle of the night, set him free, and walked him clean out of the jail house.

"Now behold, an angel of the Lord stood by him, and a light shone in the prison; and he struck Peter on the side and raised him up, saying, "Arise quickly!" And his chains fell off his hands. Then the angel said to him, "Gird yourself and tie on your sandals"; and so he did. And he said to him, "Put on your garment and follow me." So he went out and followed him, and did not know that what was done by the angel was real, but thought he was seeing a vision. When they were past the first and the second guard posts, they came to the iron gate that leads to the city, which opened to them of its own accord; and they went out and

went down one street, and immediately the angel departed from him."
Acts 12:7

Angels were working with Daniel to deliver an important message when a principality made war with Gabriel to hinder the answer from God. Michael, the archangel, showed up and defeated the hindering spirit, so Daniel could receive his answer.

"Then he said to me, "Do not fear, Daniel, for from the first day that you set your heart to understand, and to humble yourself before your God, your words were heard; and I have come because of your words. But the prince of the kingdom of Persia withstood me twenty-one days; and behold, Michael, one of the chief princes, came to help me, for I had been left alone there with the kings of Persia." Daniel 10:10-13

Jesus was in the wilderness fasting and praying for many days. He was under intense spiritual warfare as the devil brought temptation after temptation to Him. Jesus overcame every temptation because He worked the Word of God against them. After the intense battle was over, God sent supernatural strength as the angels ministered to Him. (Matthew 4:1-11) Angels are on assignment for us. We must be aware of this fact and expect them to be working on our behalf day and night!

Write a prayer for angelic assistance based out of Psalm 91 for yourself and everyone you love. Refer to it and pray it daily.

ABOUT THE AUTHOR

Pastor Felecia Wade is a powerful teacher of the Word of God. She has been in ministry since 1996. She proudly assists her husband, Apostle Tony Wade, in pastoring at *Divine Life Church*. Pastor Felecia is passionate about prayer as well as teaching young ladies and women their worth in Christ. She has ministered at various churches nationwide. She is the author of *Characteristics of Phenomenal Women* and *Memoirs of the Supernatural*. She hosts a weekly prayer broadcast on social media. She has been married to Apostle Tony since 1992. To this union, they have two adult daughters, Tonecia and Soteria who both reside in Memphis, TN.

BIBLIOGRAPHY

Zadai, Kevin. "The Agenda of Angels, What the Holy Ones Want You To Know About the Next Move of God". Shippensburg, PA: Destiny Image Publishers, Inc: 2019.